Is Anyone There?
idea by Alan Robertson
story by Deborah Manley
pictures by Rod Cole
for Catherine & James

Take 1

This book isn't finished when you buy it! It needs your own pictures fixed in behind the holes so that the faces look out at you.

Only when you have put in your pictures and fixed the 'working pages' together is your book complete.

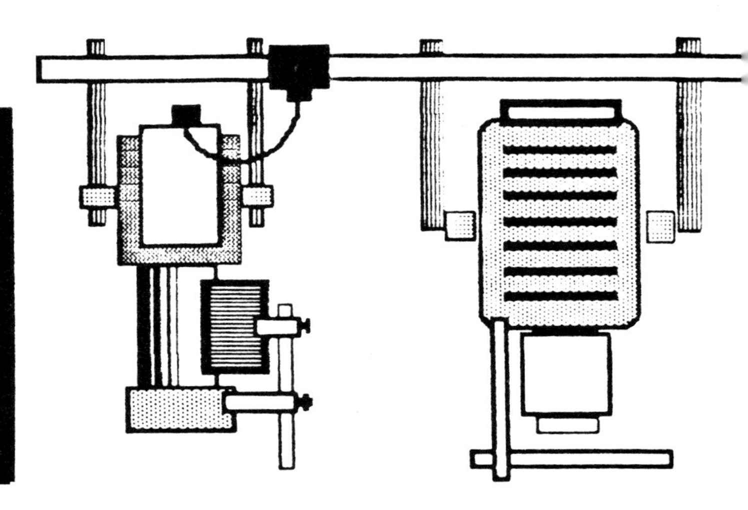

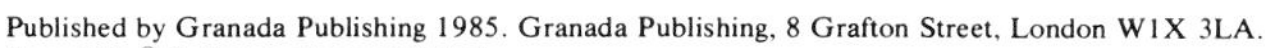

Published by Granada Publishing 1985. Granada Publishing, 8 Grafton Street, London W1X 3LA.

British Library Cataloguing in Publication Data. Manley, Deborah. Is anyone there?. — (Foto fun) I. Title II. Series 823'.914(J) PZ7.
ISBN 0-246-12675-2. Printed and bound by Graficas Reunidas, Madrid.

Author: Deborah Manley. Illustrator: Rod Cole.

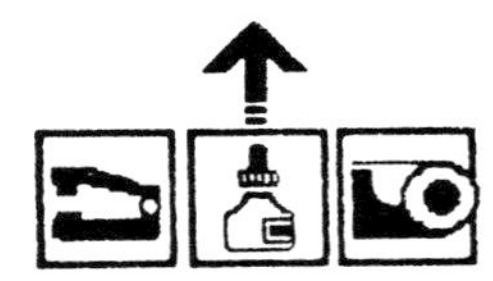

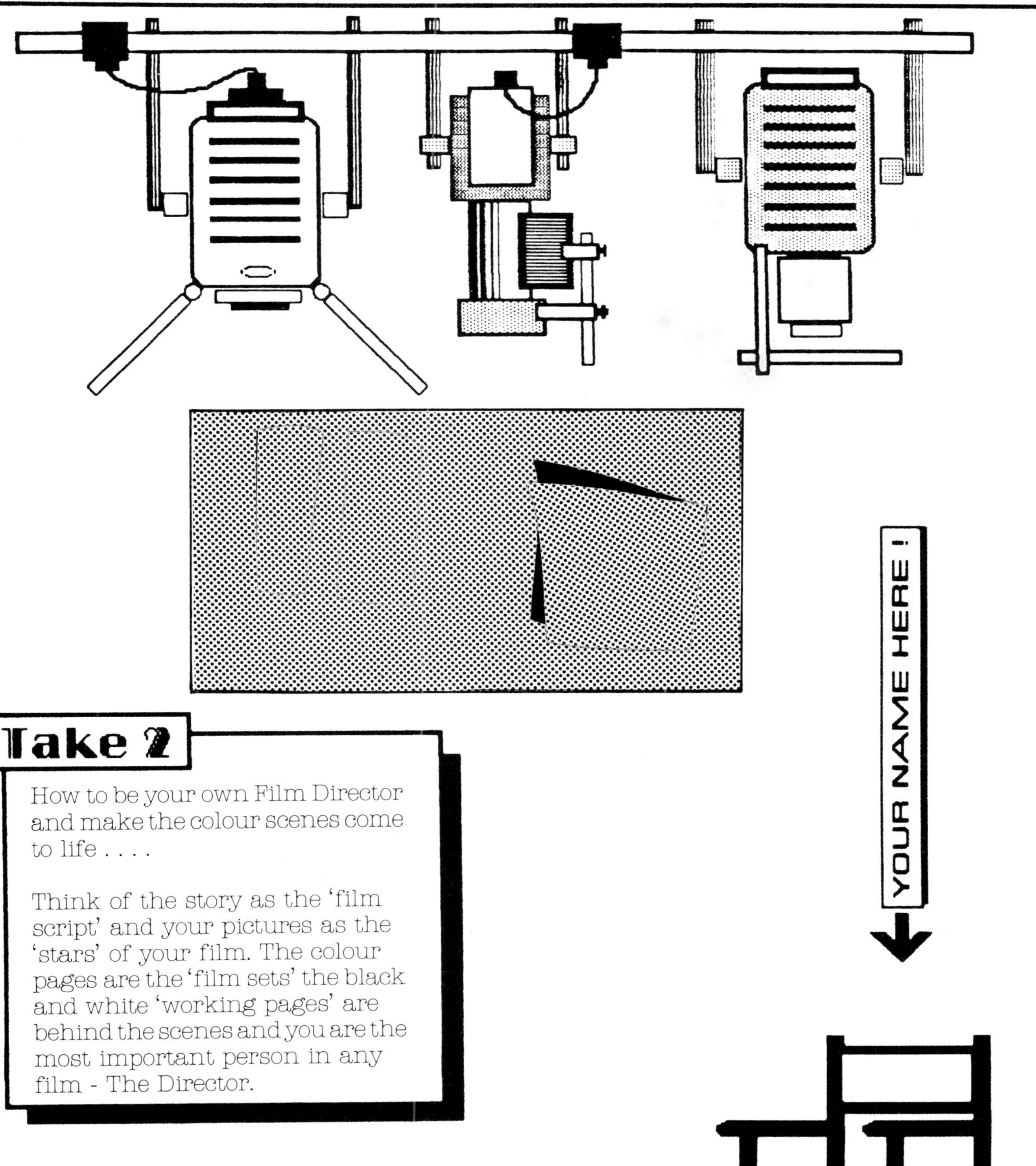

Take 2

How to be your own Film Director and make the colour scenes come to life . . . .

Think of the story as the 'film script' and your pictures as the 'stars' of your film. The colour pages are the 'film sets' the black and white 'working pages' are behind the scenes and you are the most important person in any film - The Director.

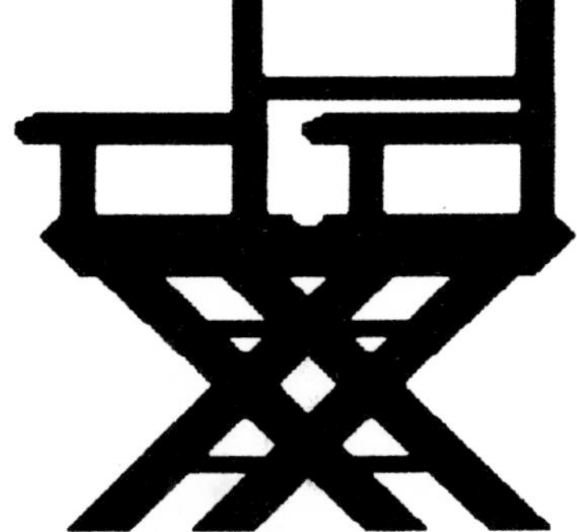

Take 3

Collect together enough pictures of faces of people and animals to fill all the 'holes' in the book. You may not have enough at first, but use what you have now and find others and add them later.

script
It was a dark and stormy night. The rain lashed down, drenching any poor creature foolish or unlucky enough to be out. The wind roared through the bare branches of the trees. Thunder rumbled behind the hills. A stage-coach trundled its unwieldy way along the rutted road across the windswept moors.
What desperate travellers could be venturing out in such a dreadful night as this?

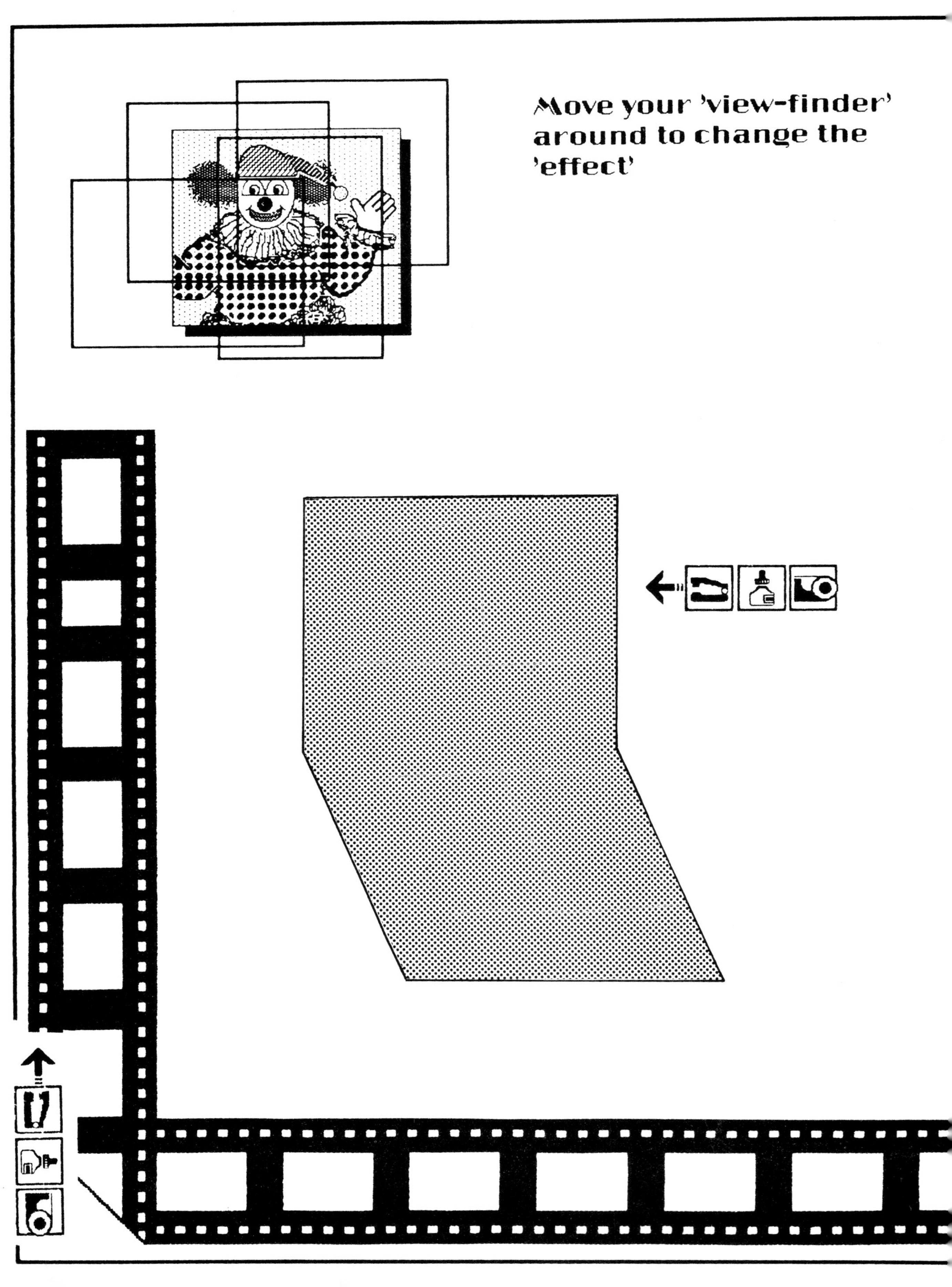
Move your 'view-finder' around to change the 'effect'

All the great Directors 'experiment' - you try now......

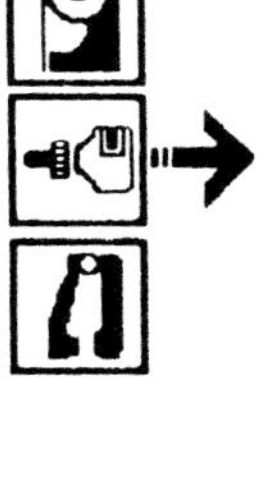

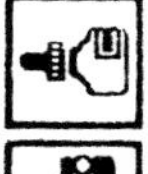

Take 4

The pictures can be photographs of your family and friends or pictures from magazines and comics - of pop stars, sports personalities, film and TV stars, politicians, animals, monsters - whatever or whoever takes your fancy.

At long last the stage-coach reached a cluster of houses huddled around an inn.

"Warmth and comfort at last!" cried the weary travellers.

They staggered out of the coach across the cobbled yard and peered in through the crooked shutters of the inn. What a weird sight met their eyes!

There, carousing inside was the strangest collection of people you could ever fear to see! The travellers fled back to the safety of the coach.
"This is no place to stay," they muttered. "Drive on!" they called to the driver.

Your 'Star' doesn't have to be in the centre of the 'frame'

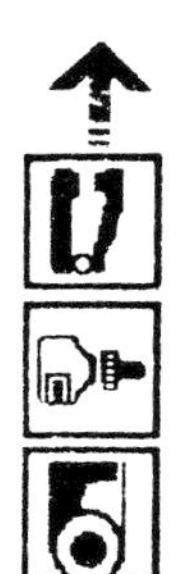

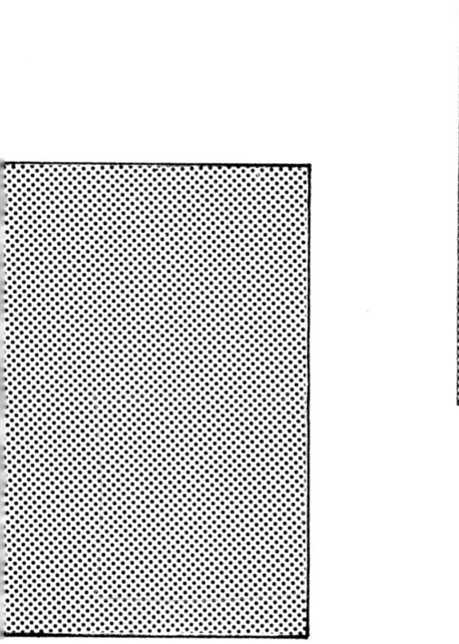

Take 5

Be sure that no one minds you using these pictures to make your book. They can, if you want, be removed later or left in the book always.

Don't worry about 'scale'

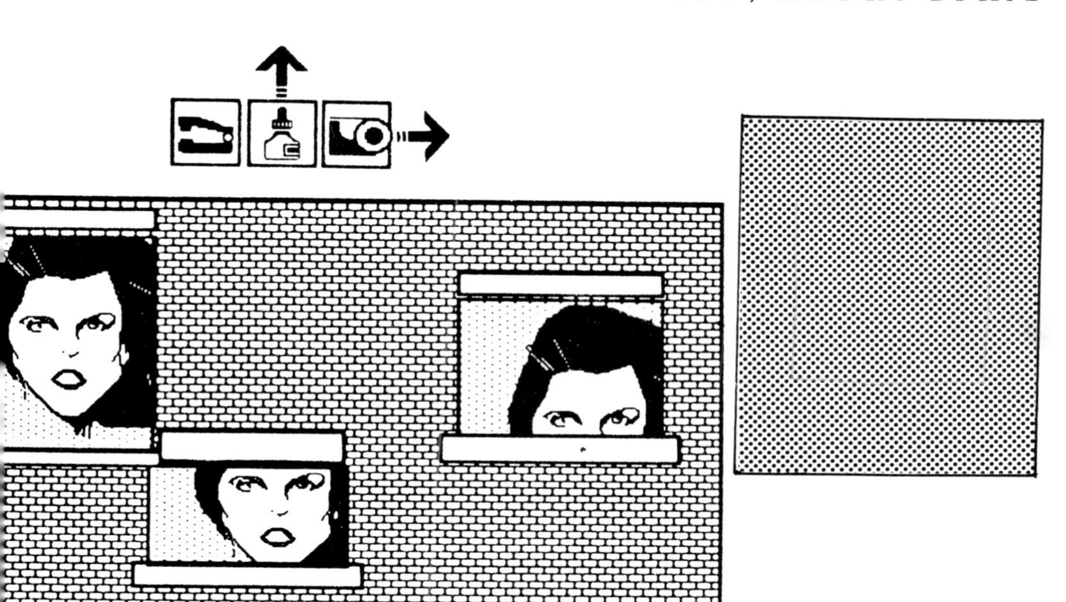

script
Off again the stage-coach trundled into the terrible night. The rain lashed down. The trees bent and groaned in the wind. The thunder rumbled ever closer. A sudden flash of lightning lit the sky.
Ahead in the gloom they saw the black hulk of a castle. Perhaps here they would find shelter from the storm.
The travellers staggered from the coach and hammered at the huge door. They waited in silence, the rain dripping from their shoulders. Was no one there?
Then high in the crumbling castle walls, shutters creaked open and faces peered down on them. Suddenly the door was flung open to reveal the most terrifying being they had ever seen. "Come in, friends, come in. You are just in time for dinner," the being welcomed them with a ghastly grin.
There was nothing for it on a night like this. Wet, weary, windswept and fearful the travellers entered, and the great door slammed behind them.

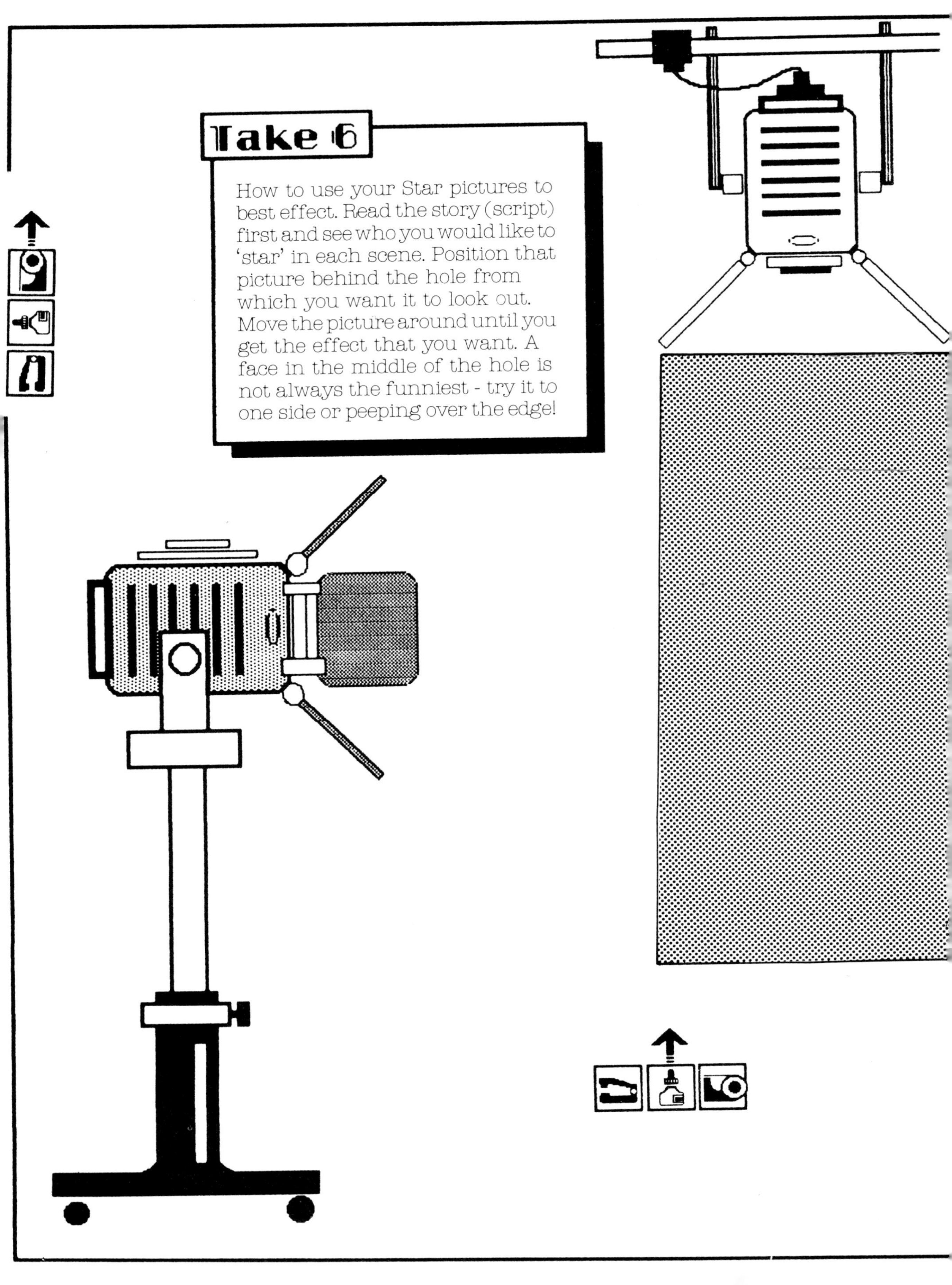
Take 6
How to use your Star pictures to best effect. Read the story (script) first and see who you would like to 'star' in each scene. Position that picture behind the hole from which you want it to look out. Move the picture around until you get the effect that you want. A face in the middle of the hole is not always the funniest - try it to one side or peeping over the edge!

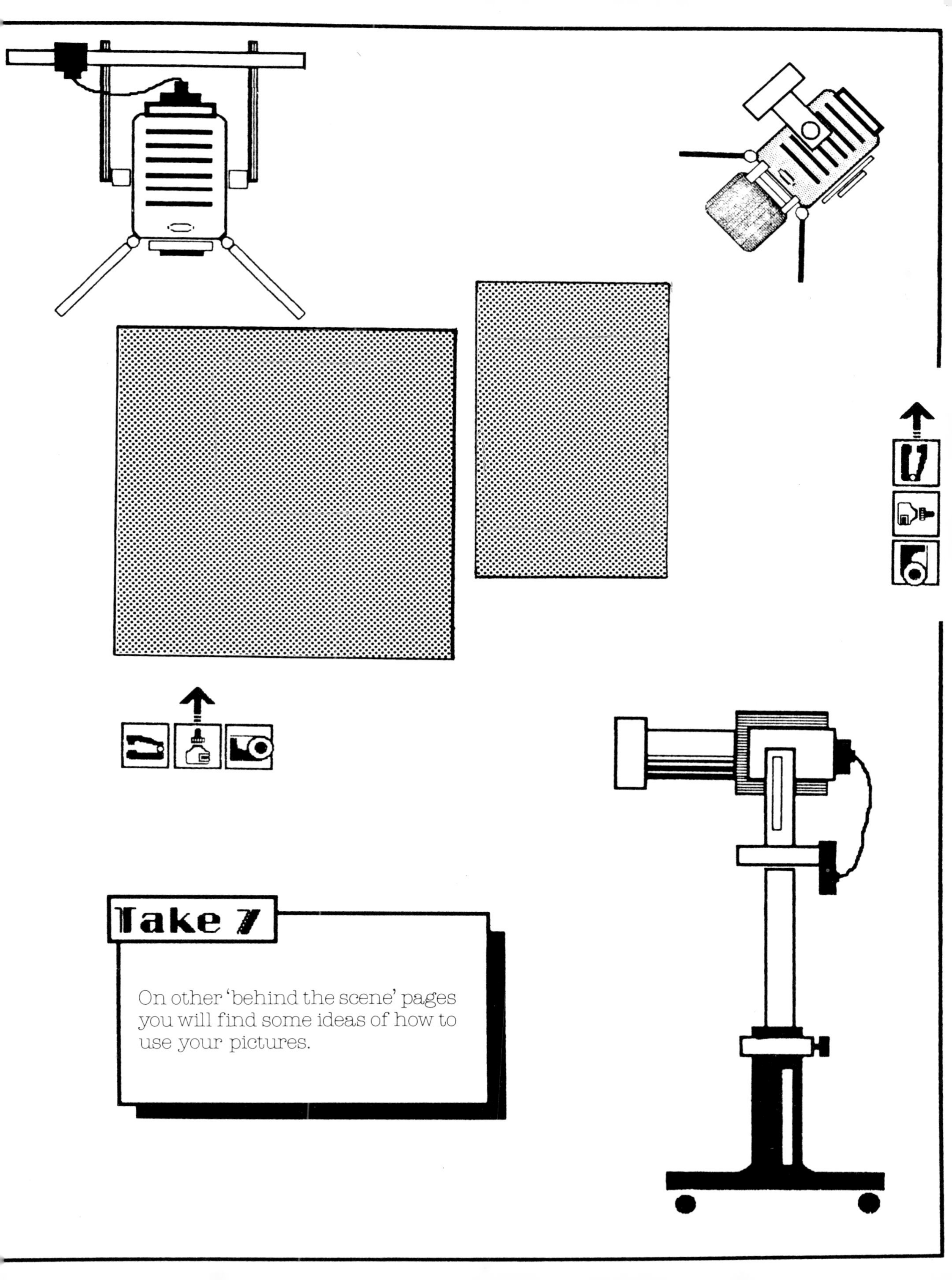
Take 7
On other 'behind the scene' pages you will find some ideas of how to use your pictures.

script
The travellers found themselves alone in a vast hall. The terrifying being had vanished.
"Is anyone there?" the travellers called.
Their voices echoed from the rafters. "Is anyone there? Anyone?"
A door banged. The shutters rattled on their hinges. The panelling creaked. A groan came from a towering suit of black armour. Faces leered out at them from around the vast hall . . . faces that grimaced and smiled at them mockingly.
"Yes, there's something here."

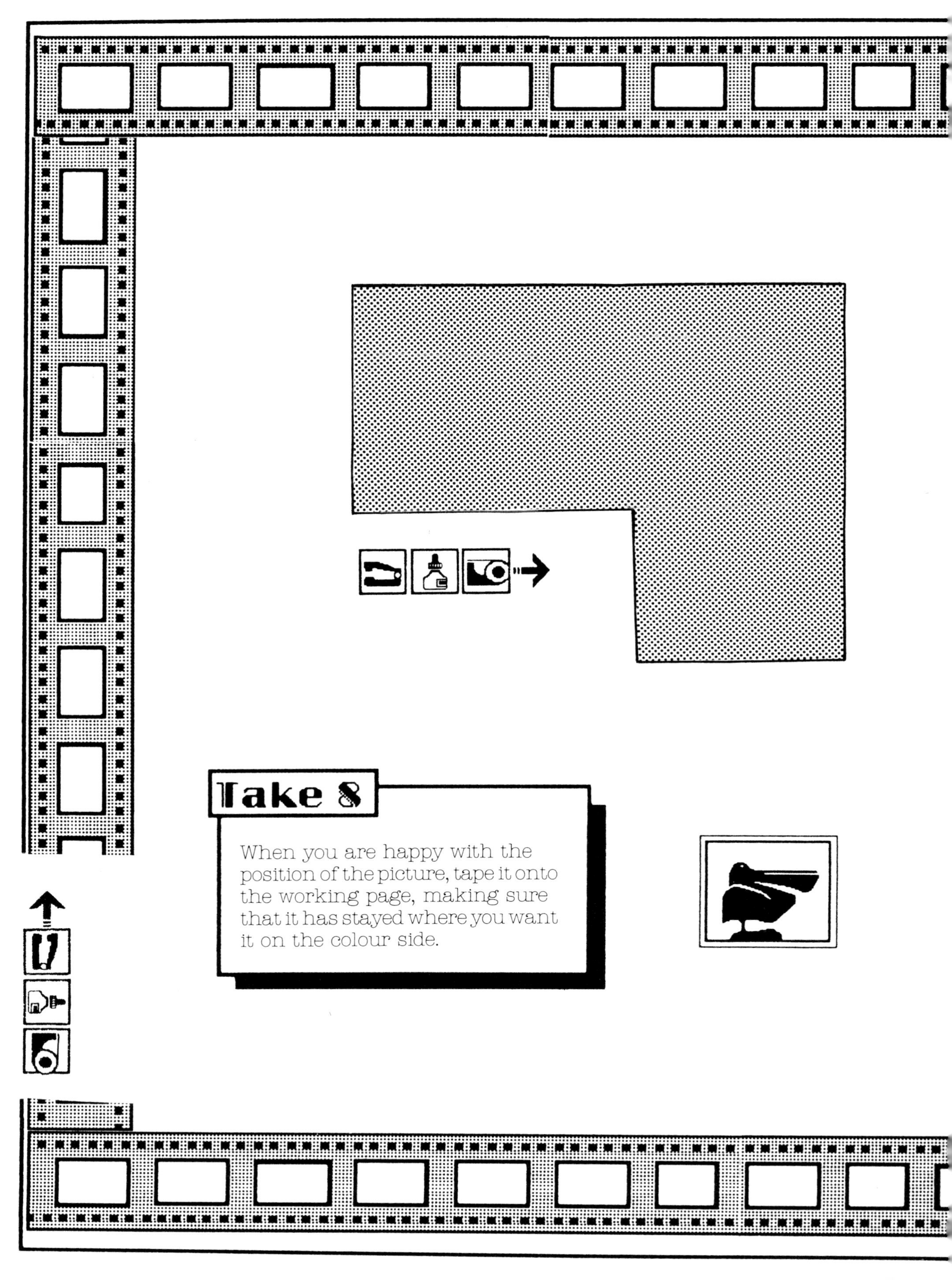

Take 8

When you are happy with the position of the picture, tape it onto the working page, making sure that it has stayed where you want it on the colour side.

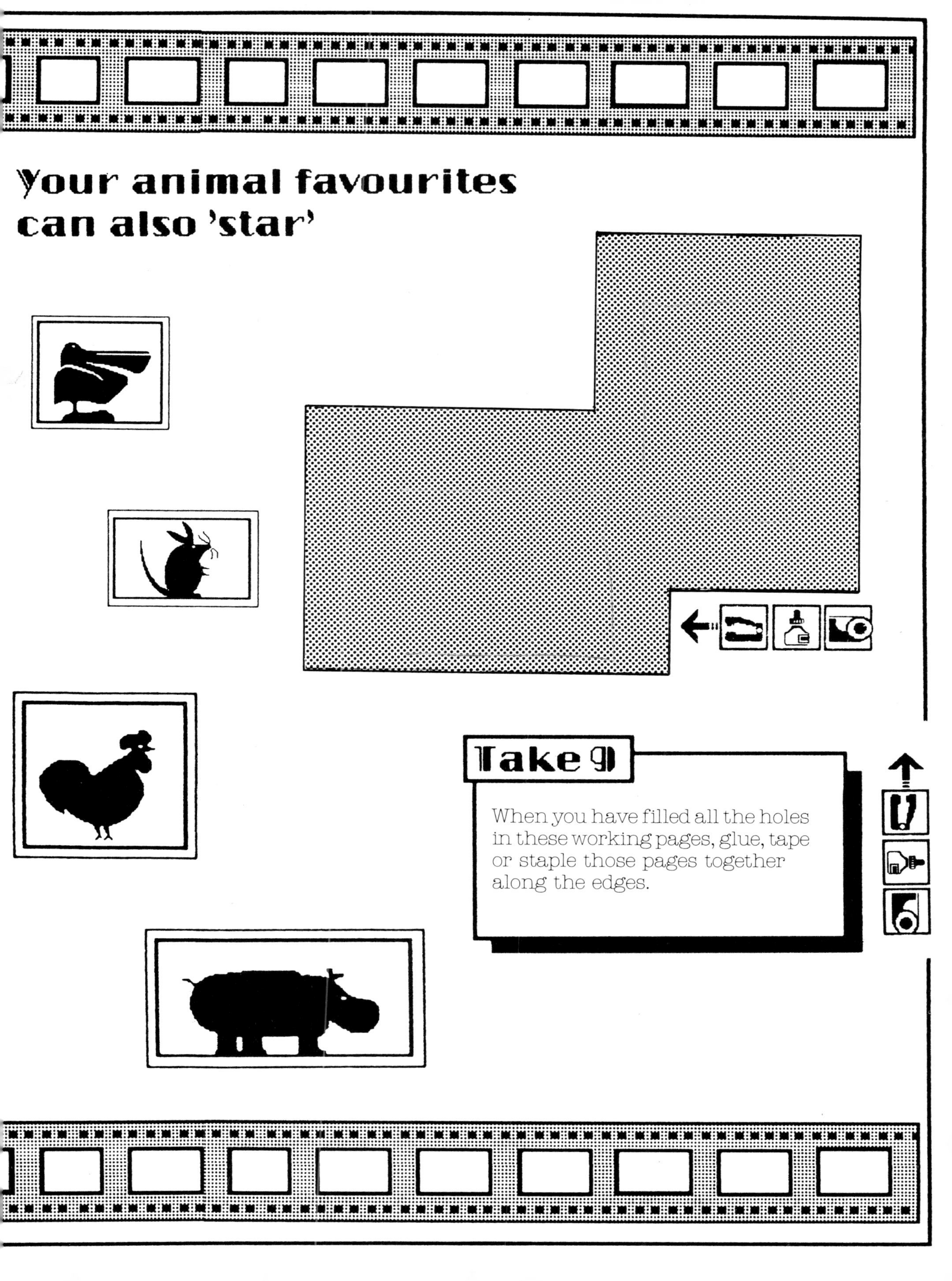

Your animal favourites can also 'star'

Take 9

When you have filled all the holes in these working pages, glue, tape or staple those pages together along the edges.

script
The travellers fled up the great staircase. Ahead of them stretched a long, dark corridor smelling of mildew and dust. One flickering candle was the only light in the gloom.
"Is anyone there?" the travellers called again.
Doors groaned open, screeching on their hinges.
Through each door yet another fearsome being peered out at them.

script
The travellers turned and rushed blindly up a twisting staircase. Up and up they dragged themselves away from the fearsome creatures down below. At last they reached another door.
In desperation they knocked and called again. "Is anyone there? Anyone?"
The door opened with a squeal and a screech. There inside was the most horrific of all the creatures they had seen.
"Yes, I am here," it wailed. "I was waiting for my dinner. Why have they sent you so late?"

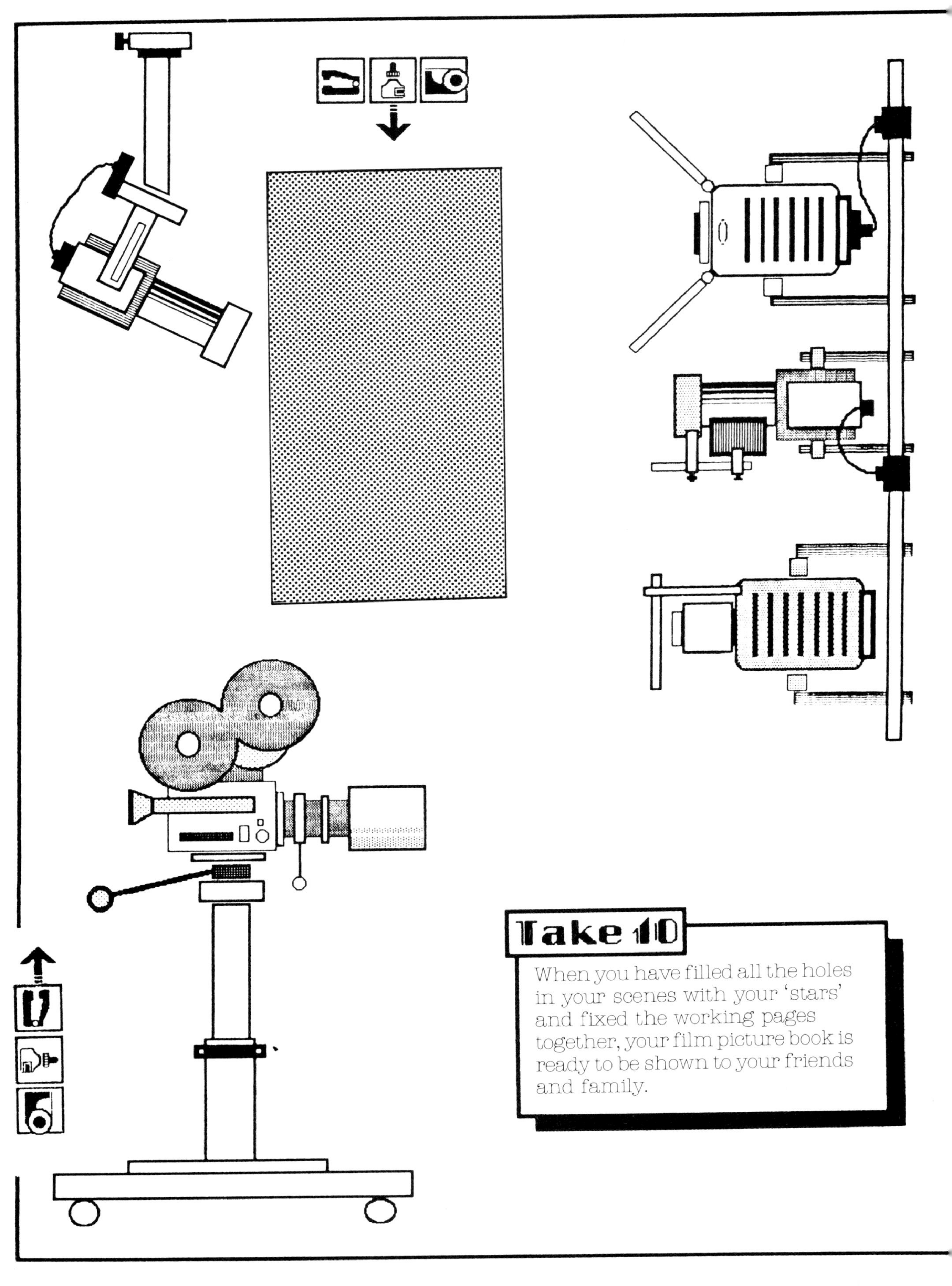
Take 10
When you have filled all the holes in your scenes with your 'stars' and fixed the working pages together, your film picture book is ready to be shown to your friends and family.

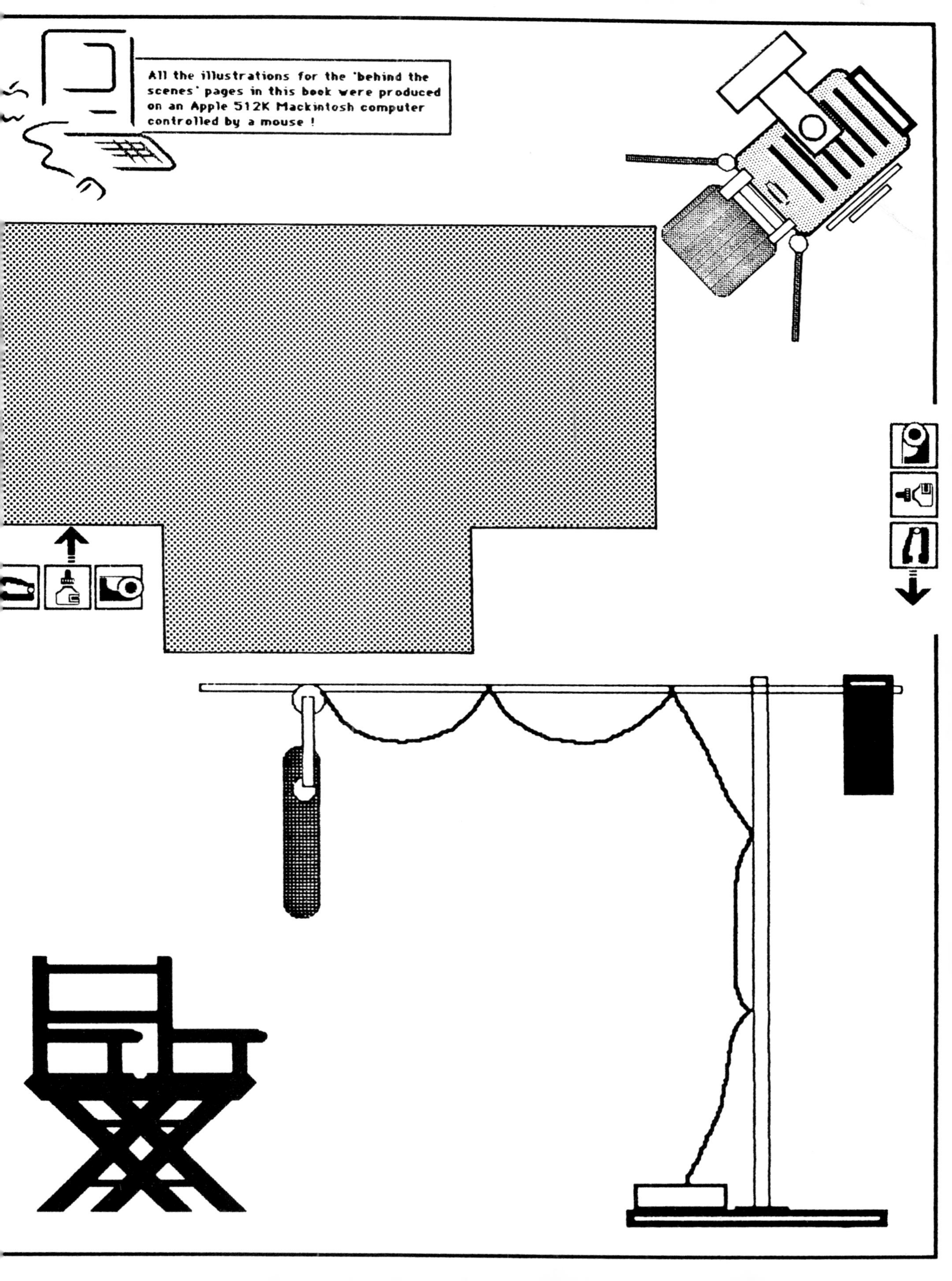
All the illustrations for the 'behind the scenes' pages in this book were produced on an Apple 512K Mackintosh computer controlled by a mouse !

script
The travellers ran. Down the twisting stairs. Along the corridor. Down the great staircase. Through the vast hall. Out through the huge door into the night and away.
As they slithered down the hill, the travellers heard behind them that terrible voice wailing, "Dinner! Is anyone there for my dinner?"